The ABC's of Parenting

WRITTEN BY

Kerby Houff

ILLUSTRATED BY

Yili Lim

Published by Dream Big Press

To my amazing and supportive wife, Meredith, and to the inspiration for this book, our four wonderful children.

-Kerby

To my husband Anthony, for this journey in life has been made all the brighter with your support, kindness, and belief in me.

-Yili

A is for Alcohol,

take the edge off with a heavy pour of your favorite drink.

B is for Bottle Service,

not the club kind, the ones that are piling up in the sink.

C is for Caffeine,

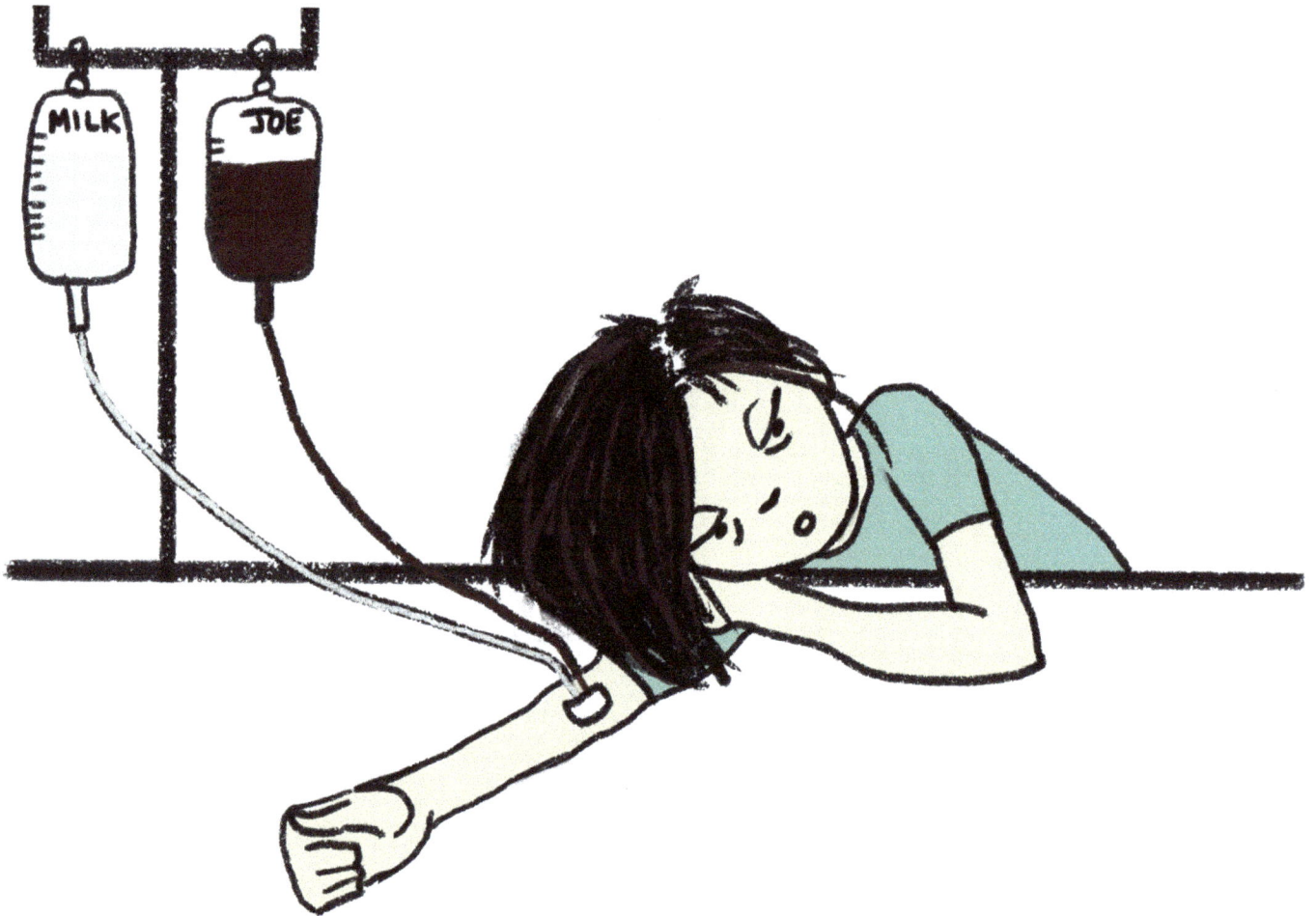

pour a cup of coffee, better make that two.

D is for **Dignity**,

doing things you said you would never do.

E is for Enthusiasm,

digging deep to show interest in each art project, every sport score.

F is for Freedom,

shackled to new responsibilities,
something you have no more.

G is for Guilt,

anguishing over every decision,
every word.

H is for Humility,

realizing some of your pre-children judging was rather absurd.

I is for Insurance,

for all the doctor visits and emergency care.

J is for Jealousy,

knowing nights out without kids
are extremely rare.

K is for Kindness,

something you need when your
child's tantrum is at a fever pitch.

L is for Love,

the feeling of being her hero that makes you feel unspeakably rich.

M is for Money,

the cost to raise and educate a child continues to spike.

N is for Nap,

that brief respite when your child sleeps and you do whatever you like.

O is for Odors,

the diapers, the many smells,
the stench.

P is for Playdate,

your new social life is sharing
(interrupted) time with another
parent on the playground bench.

Q is for Queue,

filling your streaming service with fresh content for evenings at home.

R is for Reflexes,

leaping from the couch to
investigate your child who likes to
roam.

S is for Sunscreen,

the assignment no parent wants is
to lay it on thick for a day
in the sun.

T is for Trusts (and wills),

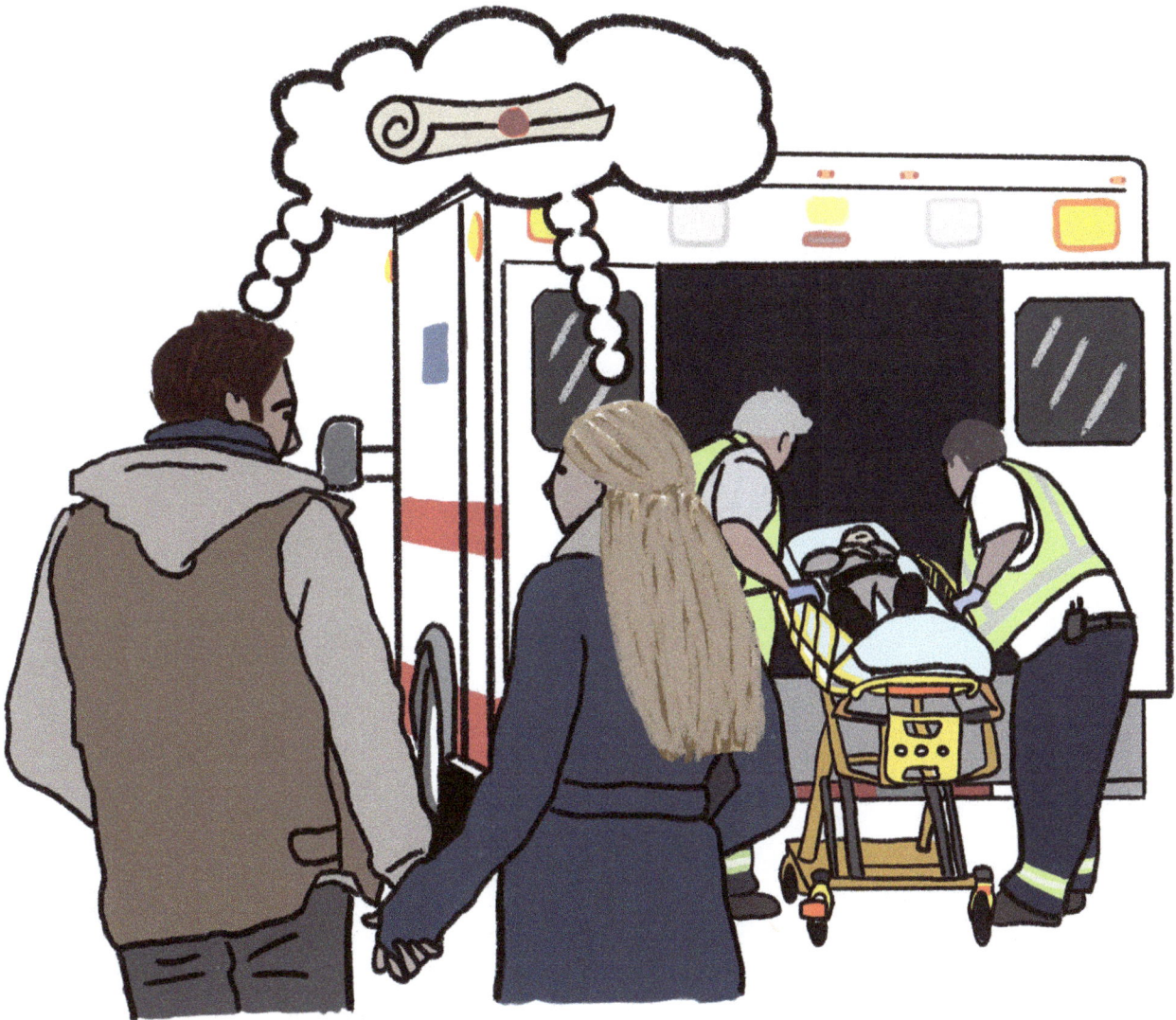

planning for your mortality is necessary, but it is not fun.

U is for Unkempt,

stepping out into public disheveled,
in a ball cap, with dry shampoo.

V is for Vulgarity,

you may hang up your curse words
and exchange "sh*t" for "doodoo".

W is for Why's,

the parade of questions and inquisitiveness that come in bunches.

X is for XOXO,

the salutation you use on the note
you insert in his bag lunches.

Y is for Years,

you start to notice when you're a parent that these pass way too fast.

Z is for Zen,

find your way to tranquility - parenting is hard but it is also a complete blast.

The End

About the Author

Kerby is a devoted father and husband, who splits his time between New York City and Virginia. This project is his first book.

About the Illustrator

Yili is an emerging artist working in Brooklyn, NY. She creates bold, colorful artwork with a surreal egde.

Visit her work at www.yililim.com

Dream Big Press books may be purchased for educational, business, or sales promotional use. For information, please email info@yililim.com.

Published in the United States of America in 2019 by Dream Big Press.

FIRST U.S. EDITION

Library of Congress Cataloging-in-Publication Data has been applied for.

ISBN 978-0-578-22108-3

Dream Big

www.ingramcontent.com/pod-product-compliance
Lightning Source LLC
Chambersburg PA
CBHW040256100426
42811CB00011B/1286